D0569116

ivardi, Anne.
ags and purses /

010.
3305222510145
a          02/17/11

# Bags and Purses

## Anne Civardi

### Photography by Sam Hare & Jane Paszkiewicz

## SEA-TO-SEA

*Mankato Collingwood London*

This edition first published in 2010 by Sea-to-Sea Publications
Distributed by Black Rabbit Books
P.O. Box 3263
Mankato, Minnesota 56002

Copyright © Sea-to-Sea Publications 2010

Printed in USA

All rights reserved.

Library of Congress Cataloging-in-Publication Data
Civardi, Anne.
  Bags and purses / Anne Civardi ; photography by Sam Hare & Jane Paszkiewicz.
     p. cm. --  (World of design)
  Includes bibliographical references and index.
    ISBN 978-1-59771-207-1 (hardcover : alk. paper)
     1.  Handbags--Juvenile literature.  I. Hare, Sam. II. Paszkiewicz, Jane. III. Title.
    TT667.C49 2010
    646.4'8--dc22

                                                2008043069

          9  8  7  6  5  4  3  2

          Published by arrangement with the Watts Publishing
          Group Ltd., London.


             Design: Rachel Hamdi and Holly Fulbrook
                  Editor: Ruth Thomson

The author would like to thank these people for the loan of
items from their collection: Shikasuki Vintage Boutique,
Primrose Hill, London NW1 8LD (www.shikasuki.com): vintage
metal butterfly bag, 4; vintage PVC vinyl poodle bag, 5;
vintage wooden box bag, 5; vintage beaded fish purse,10.
Steinberg and Tolkien: vintage box bag, 2; vintage jeweled
palace bag, 3; vintage box bag, 22. Doy Bags
(www.doybags.com): foil beltbag, 3; foil purse, 11; foil MP3
player holder, 15. Joss Graham
(www.jossgrahamgallery@btopenworld.com): silk and
sequin bag, 4; embroidered fob watch cover, 4; woven
wool purse, 5; embroidered amulet holder, 11; embroidered
fabric wallet, 18. Tyrrell Katz (www.beachfactory.com):
laminated cotton bags and towels, 4, 8. Zip••it TM
(www.zipitstyle.com): zip bag, 11.
Islington Education Library Service
(www.objectlessons.org): sequin and
mirror bag, 2, 14; Indian drawstring
bag, 3; Afghan bag, 14; Victorian
beltbag, 19; newspaper bags, 23. With special thanks to
Diana Marsh for her help and advice.

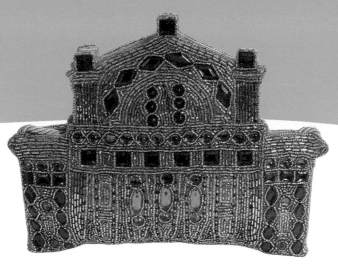

# Contents

☼ Recycled juice-pack beltbag from the Philippines

☼ Indian, embroidered silk-and-sequin drawstring bag

☼ Small fabric bee pouch from China

# Money containers

All over the world people design and create money containers, such as bags, purses, pouches, wallets, and beltbags, in many different shapes, sizes, and colors.

They may be made from beads, leather, plastic, wood, metal, paper, felt, woven camel hair, recycled juice packs, and even bottle caps.

☼ Laminated cotton beach bag from England

☼ Finely woven wool shoulder bag from Bolivia

4

*❉ Vintage, American PVC vinyl purse with appliqué poodle of cut glass stones and beads*

*❉ Bead and cowrie shell purse made in Kenya*

This book shows you bags and purses in all kinds of different styles, and various clasps and fastenings used to close them.

It will help you understand how people design and create money containers. It will show you a few simple sewing stitches so you can make some bags and purses of your own.

*❉ Embroidered fob-watch cover from Afghanistan*

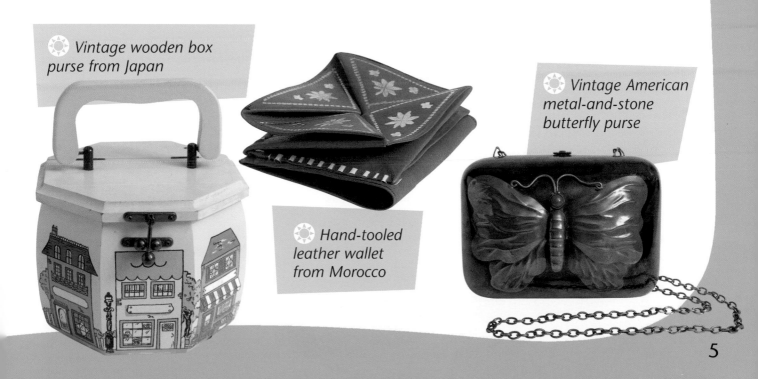

*❉ Vintage wooden box purse from Japan*

*❉ Hand-tooled leather wallet from Morocco*

*❉ Vintage American metal-and-stone butterfly purse*

5

# Drawstring bags

These bags are called drawstring bags because they open and close by pulling, or drawing, a cord, string, or strap tight.

☀ *Cotton and plastic were laminated (bonded or pressed) together to create the fabric for this English beach bag. The laminated cotton makes the bag waterproof.*

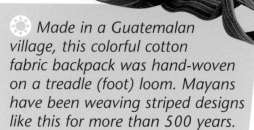

☀ *Made in a Guatemalan village, this colorful cotton fabric backpack was hand-woven on a treadle (foot) loom. Mayans have been weaving striped designs like this for more than 500 years.*

## Look closer

- The towel was designed to match the soccer motifs on the bag.

- There is a handy pocket on one side that closes with a zipper.

- The two drawstring shoulder straps allow the bag to be used as a backpack.

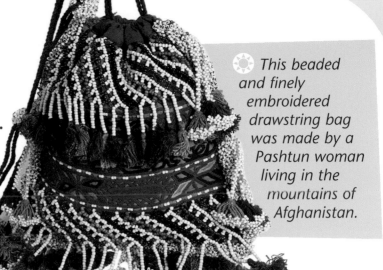

## Look closer

- This bag is made of hand-embroidered fabric.
- It is decorated with strings of glass beads.
- Tassels of colorful cotton thread are attached to the ends of the beads.

*☼ This beaded and finely embroidered drawstring bag was made by a Pashtun woman living in the mountains of Afghanistan.*

## Look closer

- The drawstring strap of this purse is held tight with a small leather strip.
- The diamond pattern was created with thin strips of white leather.
- There are several pockets around the bottom of the purse.

*☼ This Moroccan bag is made of cowhide. The hide was treated in a vat of pink dye and pigeon droppings.*

*☼ The little fish of this fabric Chinese wallet is for coins. The big one is for paper money. In China, fish are a symbol of good luck.*

# Making a drawstring bag

You will need

**1** Cut out a paper pattern (template) 16 x 37in (40 x 94cm). Pin it to the fabric and cut around it.

- 19in (0.5m) laminated cotton fabric
- paper ● scissors ● pins and a needle ● thread ● a big safety pin
- 3ft (1m) cord

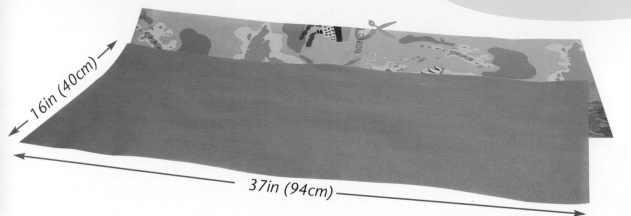

← 16in (40cm) →

—— 37in (94cm) ——

**2** With the shiny side facing down, fold over and pin 1½in (4cm) at either end.

1½in (4 cm)

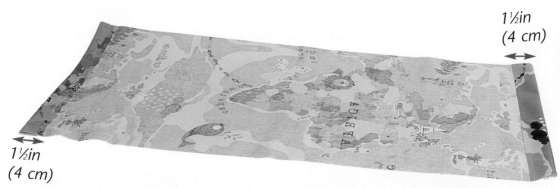

1½in (4 cm)

1½in (4cm)

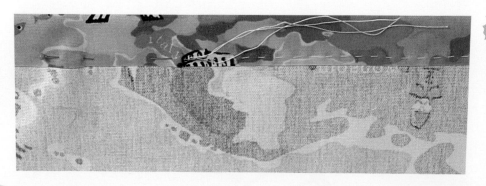

**3** Using running stitch (see page 30), sew along both folds, ½in (1cm) from the edges. Remove the pins as you go.

8

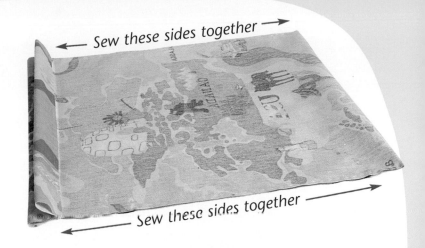

*Sew these sides together*

*Sew these sides together*

**4** Fold the fabric in half with the shiny sides together. Sew the sides together, ½in (1cm) from the edge, until you reach the folded ends.

**5** Turn the bag so that the shiny side faces out. Knot both ends of the cord. Poke a big safety pin through one knot. Thread the pin through the gap in the folded ends of the bag.

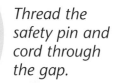

*Thread the safety pin and cord through the gap.*

**6** Once the cord is threaded through, take off the safety pin and knot the ends together. Pull the cord to gather the top of your beach bag tight.

*Knot the ends of the cord together.*

9

# Purses and pouches

Purses and pouches are small so they can fit into a purse or pocket. They are used to carry coins and have fastenings that stop the coins from falling out.

*Created in a village high up in the Himalayan mountains of Nepal, this felt pencil case was handmade from sheep's wool. Nepalese people also use felt to make rugs.*

## Look closer

- The pouch is made from a square of fabric.
- It is embroidered with a geometric pattern.
- Pushing the glass bead up or down the cords opens or closes the pouch.

*This pouch was made by the Banjara tribe in India. It was used to hold an amulet. An amulet is thought to bring good luck and give protection.*

- This wallet is beaded on both sides in the shape of a stripy fish with a tail, mouth, eyes, and fins.
- The lines of beads are designed to look like tiny fish scales.

*Women in the Philippines make purses and wallets from recycled foil juice packs. They weave strips of foil together to create a colorful pattern.*

*Created in Korea about 40 years ago, this beaded wallet has a clasp made of two metal balls that snap together.*

**Look closer**

- The bag below starts out as a long flat zipper made from two different colors.
- When it is completely zipped up, it forms a bag with a handle.

*This zipper bag was designed in the USA and won the Product of the Year award in Boston. The biggest Zipit bag has a zipper that is more than 270 inches (690 cm) long.*

# Making a perfect pouch

## You will need

- soft cotton fabric ● paper
- scissors ● needle and pins ● thread
- beads and sequins ● 40in (100cm)
  thin cord ● a large bead

**1** Cut a paper template, 5 x 5in (12 x 12cm). Fold the fabric in half and pin the template on top.

*paper template*

*5in (12cm)*

*5in (12cm)*

**2** Cut around the template, so you have two pieces of fabric, exactly the same size.

*Use double thread. Sew about ½in (1cm) from the edge.*

**3** With the fabric the right way up, use a backstitch (see page 30) to sew the two squares together, about ½in (1cm) from the edges.

*Tip: The fabric will only fray up to where you have backstitched.*

**4** Make five bead and sequin tassels, each about 3in (8cm) long.

**5** As you finish each tassel, sew it onto the fabric square, as shown.

*Tip: Make sure you sew the bead tassels inside the line of backstitching.*

**6** Cut four pieces of cord, each 10in (25cm) long. Knot one end of each piece.

**7** Poke a small hole in each corner of the fabric square, just inside the line of backstitching. Push a piece of cord through each hole. Thread the four pieces of cord through the big bead and knot the ends together.

*Tip: Push the bead down to close your pouch. You could use it to hold a good luck charm.*

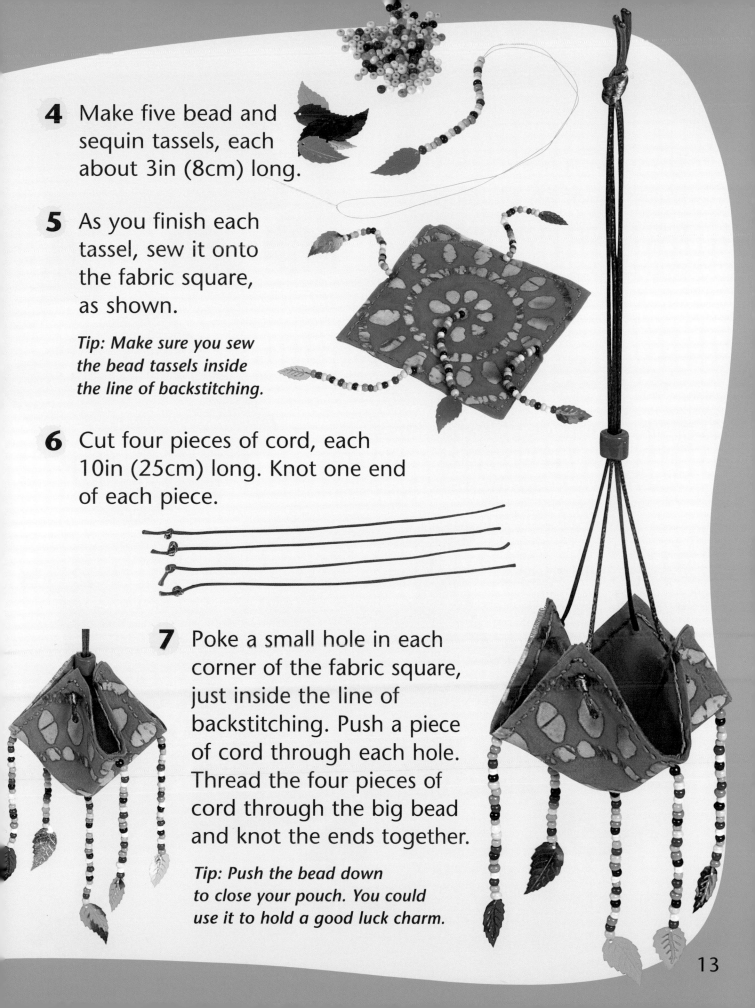

# Envelope bags

These bags are made in the style of an envelope with a flap that opens and closes.

*Both of these bags have loop fastenings. The one on the embroidered Afghan bag above loops over a tassel. The one on the Moroccan silk bag loops over a crocheted silk button.*

## Look closer

- The embroidered bag below is decorated with sequins, tiny mirrors, and glass beads to make it sparkle.

- A diamond pattern has been created with gold thread.

- There are rows of small white shells sewn on the bag.

*This antique bag from Pakistan was created from a large square of finely hand-embroidered and decorated cloth.*

*Created in England, this envelope bag is made from cowhide that has been dyed bright pink.*

Look closer

- The big turquoise leather button is a special design feature of this pink bag.
- The turquoise stitching matches the button and contrasts well with the pink cowhide.

Look closer

- The jewelry roll below has been edged with silk piping.
- It has two zipped pockets to hold jewelry.
  - The rolled-up bag can be tied together with silk ribbons.

*Used to hold an MP3 player, this recycled juice pack bag was made in the Philippines. It has a long shoulder strap and a Velcro fastening.*

*Used especially for holding small pieces of jewelry, this English jewelry roll is made from printed silk.*

# Making an envelope bag

## You will need

- 16in (40cm) wool fabric
- 16in (40cm) cotton fabric
- paper ● scissors ● thread
- needle and pins ● glue
- sequins and beads ● cord

**1** Using a paper template, 12 x 12in (30 x 30cm), cut one square of wool fabric and one cotton square.

12in (30cm)

12in (30cm)

**2** Lay the cotton square on top of the wool square with the right sides facing. Sew them together, using a running stitch (see page 30). Leave about 4in (10cm) unsewn, close to one corner, as shown.

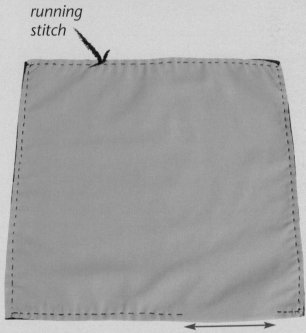

*running stitch*

*Leave 4in (10cm) open.*

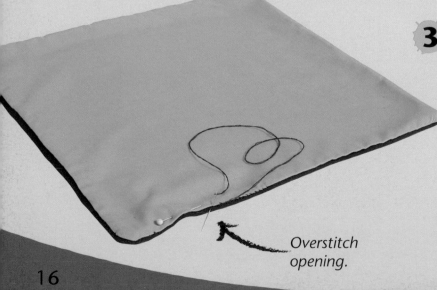

*Overstitch opening.*

**3** Turn the bag the right way out, through the opening you have left unsewn. Ask an adult to iron the fabric and then oversew (see page 30) the opening closed. This is called *bagging*.

**4** Fold three corners of the fabric over so they meet in the middle. Sew the two bottom edges together to form an envelope.

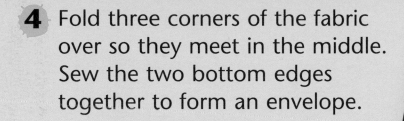

*sew along folds*

**5** Glue or sew beads and sequins on to the outside of the bag. Sew on a loop of cord. Loop it over a big sequin or sew on a button to fasten the bag.

*sequins and beads*

*Tip: You could make sequin and bead tassels, like these, for the corners of your bag.*

17

# Wallets and beltbags

Wallets have compartments designed to hold paper money, credit cards, and coins. Beltbags have loops for belts, or straps that fit around the waist.

*The pattern on this Moroccan leather wallet was created with a special tool. This is called hand-tooling. There is a snap pocket for coins and a section for paper money.*

**Look closer**

- The wallet below has two pockets for coins and cards and a long one for paper.
  - It folds in two and has a flap which closes with small snap fasteners.

*This old cloth wallet was created by a woman from the Pashtun tribe of Afghanistan. Pashtuns are famous for their fine, colorful embroidery.*

There are two loops at the back of this Indian cotton bag to hold a belt, so that it can be used as a beltbag.

In the 1800s, women hung small coin bags, like this crocheted silk one, from their belts.

**Look closer**

- The coin bag opposite only holds a few coins. These are dropped in through a small opening.
- Two rings slide over the opening to stop the coins from falling out.

**Look closer**

- A large pocket has been sewn onto the front of this belt bag. There is a smaller zipper pocket above it.
- The belt fastens at the back with Velcro.
- The woven camel hair has a black cotton lining.

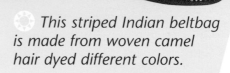

This striped Indian beltbag is made from woven camel hair dyed different colors.

# Making a wallet beltbag

5in (12cm)

5 in (12cm)

7in (18cm)

10½in (27cm)

## You will need

- 12in (0.3m) felt fabric
- 19in (0.5m) fake leather fabric
- newspaper • scissors • glue
- a needle and thread
- self-adhesive Velcro
- a belt

**1** Using a paper template, 5 x 7in (12 x 18cm), cut a rectangle of felt. With another template, 10½in x 5in (27 x 12cm), cut a rectangle of fake leather.

**2** Glue the felt onto the fake leather close to the edges. Leave the top edge open to make a felt pocket for paper money.

Leave open.

Glue these edges together.

Glue these edges together.

Glue the en togethe

**3** Fold up the felt end of the rectangle about 3½in (9cm). Overstitch (see page 30) the folded sides together to make a pocket for coins.

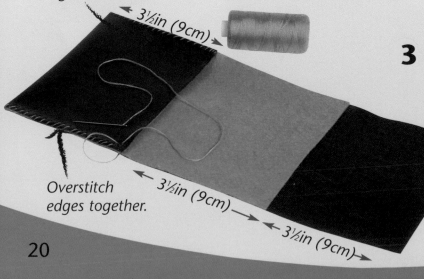

Overstitch edges together.

3½in (9cm)

Overstitch edges together.

3½in (9cm)

3½in (9cm)

**4** Fold the wallet in three, as shown. Glue three leather and felt squares as decoration to the top flap.

**5** Cut two 2½in (6cm) strips of self-adhesive Velcro, one hook side and one loop side. Stick them in place, as shown. Press them together to fasten the wallet.

*self-adhesive Velcro*

**6** Glue a strip of fake leather, 2 x 3in (5 x 8cm) to the back of the wallet as the loop for your belt.

*belt loop*

*Tip: You can use the wallet by itself or as a beltbag.*

21

# Recycled bags

In many parts of the world people recycle materials, such as boxes, fabric scraps, newspaper, bottle tops, and even old records, to turn into useful bags.

☀ *This purse was made in Kenya from recycled bottle caps attached to a wire frame. The handles are made of coiled wire.*

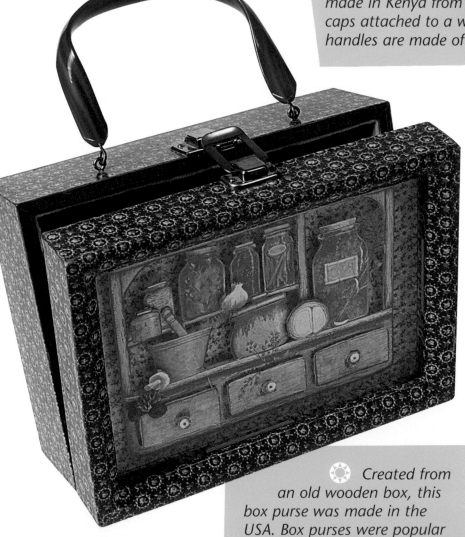

☀ *Created from an old wooden box, this box purse was made in the USA. Box purses were popular in the 1960s and 1970s.*

## Look closer

- Paper jars stand on a kitchen shelf inside the plastic window on the lid of this box purse.

- The purse has a hinged lid, a plastic handle, and a metal clasp.

- A pattern of paper circles and flowers covers the outside of the box.

*A group of women in South Africa earn a living by making rag shoulder bags like this from old t-shirts.*

## Look closer

- The shoulder bag is made by pushing and knotting strips of old t-shirts through holes in burlap.

- Because the knots of fabric look like kernels of corn, the group of women who make them are called "Mielie," which means "corn" in Swahili.

*In India, newpapers are recycled into bags like these. The money raised from selling them helps pay for street children in Delhi to go to school, instead of pulling rickshaws or polishing shoes.*

*Two old records have been included in the design of this funky plastic and metal purse.*

# Making a disco-box bag

**1** Take the label off the plastic container. Ask an adult to poke a hole into each end of the lid, as shown.

## You will need

- an empty plastic container
- scissors • gift wrapping paper
- acrylic paint and a paintbrush
- plastic jewels, scraps of lace, ribbons of sequins and ribbon
- glue • 19in (0.5m) cord

**2** Cover the lid with two layers of acrylic paint. Leave it to dry.

**3** Cut a strip of gift wrapping paper big enough to fit around the box. Glue it on.

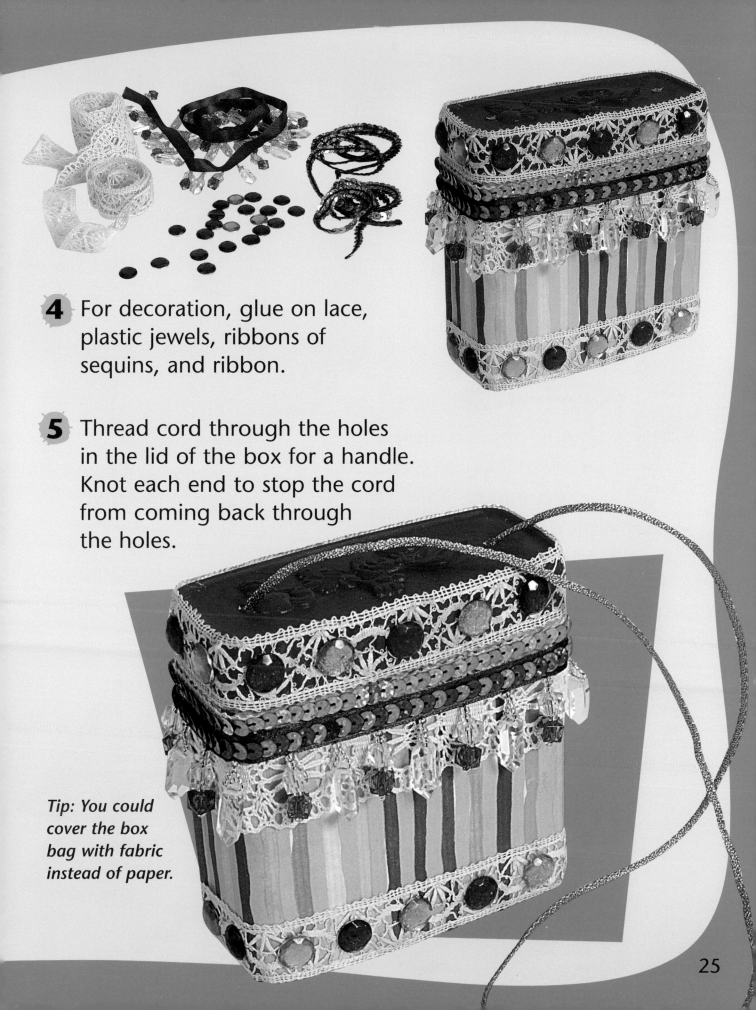

**4** For decoration, glue on lace, plastic jewels, ribbons of sequins, and ribbon.

**5** Thread cord through the holes in the lid of the box for a handle. Knot each end to stop the cord from coming back through the holes.

*Tip: You could cover the box bag with fabric instead of paper.*

# Appliqué bags

All these bags and purses have been decorated with separate pieces of material sewn or glued on top of them. This technique is called appliqué.

## Look closer

- The flower decorations on the envelope bag below are made from triangles and circles of felt.
- The bag is decorated with blanket stitching (see page 30).
- The bow was created by braiding three thin felt strips.

*Created in China, this wallet is made from pink and green plastic with a metal clasp that snaps shut. The high-heeled shoe was machine-stitched onto the front.*

*A sturdy metal snap fastener closes this felt envelope bag.*

- This shoulder bag is appliquéd with pieces of old embroidered fabric from India.

- A wide fabric strip has been sewn on to look like a belt. The pockets are both edged with thin strips.

- The bag is lined with a bright pink cotton fabric.

*An old pair of blue jeans was used to design this shoulder bag.*

**Look closer**

- A dog's ears, eyes, red tongue, and black nose was appliquéd onto the shoulder bag below.

- It was sewn on with a blanket stitch (see page 30).

*This shoulder bag from England is made of felt. Felt is created from sheep's wool and other animal fibers. These fibers turn into a fabric when they are rubbed together in warm, soapy water.*

# Making an appliqué bag

## You will need

- 19in (50cm) felt in two different colors ● small pieces of felt
- paper ● scissors
- pins and a needle ● thread
- glue ● 19in (50cm) thin ribbon

**1** Using a paper template 14 x 9½in (36 x 24cm), cut two colored felt rectangles.

14in (36cm)

9½in (24cm)

*Use double thread to blanket stitch around edges.*

**2** Pin one felt rectangle on top of the other. Sew them together with blanket stitch (see page 30).

**3** Fold up 5in (12cm) of one end of the felt rectangle to form a pocket. Glue or sew the edges together, as shown.

*Glue or sew edges together.*

9½in (24cm)

5in (12cm)

5in (12cm)

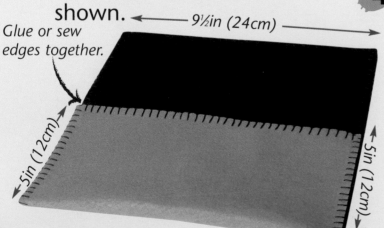

*Glue or sew edges together.*

**4** Using a paper template the size of a mug base, cut two felt circles. Use a smaller template to cut two more felt circles.

**5** Cut each felt circle in half and in half again, so you have four quarters. Cut each quarter in half to make eight triangles of felt from each circle.

**6** Glue the triangles of felt onto the bag to look like flowers. Glue felt circles on to the middle of each flower.

*Tip: You can use as many or as few felt triangles as you like to form the flowers.*

**7** Sew two pieces of ribbon onto the bag, as shown. Tie them together to fasten the bag.

*Tip: It is best to use fabric that doesn't fray when you appliqué.*

# Handy hints

You need to learn these simple stitches to make the projects in this book. To start, thread a needle and knot one end of the thread.

## Running stitch

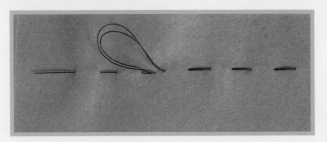

Make small stitches by pushing a threaded needle in and out of the fabric. Keep the stitches and spaces as even as possible. Finish off by sewing a couple of stitches on top of each other.

## Backstitch

Make a stitch and a space. Take the needle back over the space and bring it out the same distance in front of the thread. Repeat this, ending with two backstitches on top of each other.

## Overstitch

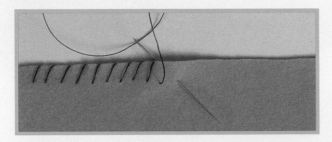

Make diagonal stitches over the raw edge of the fabric. Try to space them equally and make them all the same length. Be careful not to pull the stitches too tight. This stitch helps to stop fabric from fraying.

## Blanket stitch

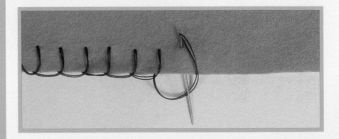

Close to the edge, push the needle from the front of the fabric to the back, with the point of the needle coming out in front of the loop made by the thread. Pull the needle and thread through until the blanket stitch is flat against the fabric.

Purses, bags, and wallets are designed with all sorts of different clasps and fastenings. Look through the book to find which of these fastenings are used on which bag, wallet, or purse.

*Metal ball clasp*

*Zipper*

*Velcro*

*Plastic belt clasp*

*Bead and cord*

*Drawstring*

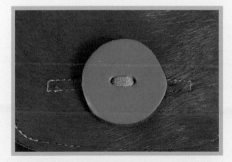

*Button and button hole*

*Metal rings*

*Suitcase clasp*

*Loop over button*

*Metal snap fastener*

*Ribbon*

# Glossary

**amulet** a charm worn on the body thought to have a magic power to protect against harm or injury

**crochet** needlework in which loops of thread or yarn are woven together using a hooked needle

**embroider** to create a design on fabric with needlework

**lining** the fabric used to cover the inside of something, such as a bag, purse, or dress

**motif** a figure or shape that is repeated in a design

**template** a pattern, in this case made of paper, that is used to make an exact copy of an object or shape

# Index